A Little Past Now and Then

"Late Night Dreamer" and Other Poems of Romance Left Behind

Steven J. Bowers

outskirts
press

A Little Past Now and Then
"Late Night Dreamer" and Other Poems of Romance Left Behind
All Rights Reserved.
Copyright © 2019 Steven J. Bowers
v2.0

This is a work of fiction. The events and characters described herein are imaginary and are not intended to refer to specific places or living persons. The opinions expressed in this manuscript are solely the opinions of the author and do not represent the opinions or thoughts of the publisher. The author has represented and warranted full ownership and/or legal right to publish all the materials in this book.

This book may not be reproduced, transmitted, or stored in whole or in part by any means, including graphic, electronic, or mechanical without the express written consent of the publisher except in the case of brief quotations embodied in critical articles and reviews.

Outskirts Press, Inc.
http://www.outskirtspress.com

Paperback ISBN: 978-1-9772-1453-9
Hardback ISBN: 978-1-9772-1454-6

Cover Photo © 2019 www.gettyimages.com. All rights reserved - used with permission.

Outskirts Press and the "OP" logo are trademarks belonging to Outskirts Press, Inc.

PRINTED IN THE UNITED STATES OF AMERICA

Contents

The Debts We Bear	1
Your Picture	2
She Was Spring	3
It's Over	4
Words Often Fail Me	5
The Rose	6
She Was Beautiful	7
I Met A Girl	10
Those Who Have Never Loved	11
Late at Night	12
Her Place	13
As Time Creeps Up	14
Want	15
Searching	16
Ghosts	17
Late Night Dreamer	18
Even Though	19
If Life Was Simple	20
The Days Are Long	22
It's Alright	23
Days and Nights	24
I Hear Your Thoughts	25
The Old Man	26
Little Town Church	27
Imperfect	28
Another Time	29

The Girl in the Diner	30
V-day	31
The Flame	32
Later Years	33
A Day in the Life	34
One Short Life	35
August Moon	36
Fifth of Nowhere	37
In Plain Sight	38
An Ode to Jessie	39
Remember	40
Christmas Blue	41
My Christmas Dream	42
Tell Me	43
Coffee to Go	44
On the Counter	45
The Internet	46
Complaining	47
On Her Knees	48
Comfort	49

The Debts We Bear

The Debt We Bear
We carry them like chains
As we tread through life seemingly alone
At the end of the journey they resurface
As regret or shame or life's unfulfilled promises
Truly we will find a way to shed them
And live what's left with no remorse
But the memories haunt and the chains tighten
With time to reflect and wonder.
It seems so hard to forget...
Those forks in the road...
The one we let get away
Decisions made seem heavy in retrospect.
Quietly now we revisit, contemplate, and ponder.
What could have been. If only if…
It's all a useless endeavor.
Too late to change the clock.
Still the nagging past haunts us.
Inward we look for answers.
Time torments the lonely.

Your Picture

Your Picture
Appeared on my screen today
Apparently after some quick clicks and keyboard strokes
That I was unaware I had even made
And there you were.
It took me by surprise, I guess.
My hands simply called you up on their very own.
But I left your image remain for a while
As I went about so many other things.
Like missing you. Replaying your laughter in my mind and remembering
The touch of your sweet caress and the way your smile melted all my cares.
Before you went away you were my life. The love I had always wanted.
Yes, I left your picture remain there and I guess I don't have it in me
To make it go away.

She Was Spring

She was Spring
I was Fall.
She was like flowers and easy music and hard rain
I was nothing like that at all.
She liked early morning coffee on the front porch
I relished in late night whiskey and the crackle of fire under the moon.
She was light laughter and silly poses. A warm breeze through the April fields.
I was moody and brooding... watching the horizon for something ominous.
We were opposites. Different in almost all respects and yet...
Her smile melted me and her laughter soothed me as I took her all in.
I never knew what she saw in me or why she stayed...
Until the end... but she did.
And now I regret not giving her more... of me... of a better life...
But I feel her presence in a soft wind that kisses my cheek as I think back...
And miss her……...

It's Over

It's over it seems
And we are both left a little confused
A little bitter and a whole lot of hurt
Blame does not help
Tears come unannounced
And sadness abounds.
It's over it seems
As words are depleted
Yet emotions run strong
Is it a bond that's broken?
Or one that should ever run long
It's over it seems
Or so it would appear
Cry not
For we loved so strong
And for that we should be forever grateful

Words Often Fail Me

Words often fail me.

Emotions way too strong

Wanting to reach out

Left with a dull, plaintive face

Just know you are everything

And I am here

I would move mountains for you

If I were able

Not sure you would notice

Or appreciate

Still, who can help how they feel

Or who they love

I'll wait in the wings

In case you call.

The Rose

I picked up a rose
And carried it through town.
People stared and I felt self-conscious for having it..
But they must've thought "he's sweet on some girl"
And so I walked the considerable distance
Careful of it so as not to bend or tear any of it's
Precious petals or break its thorny stem.
I thought of how I would hide it behind my back.
When I arrive and before I give it to her.
She'll be surprised as I've never done this before.
We'll both blush as we stare at each other.
Perhaps she will kiss my cheek.
But she has never kissed me before.
Maybe…
This rose will work.

She Was Beautiful

She was beautiful.
But not like a rose.
And not like a picture I suppose
But she was beautiful like a quiet sunset eve
In a fall colored woods or ever rolling field of deep carpet green.
Her features were feminine with nicely padded places
Where ladies often are.
Her soul and presence would soothe and deliver me down from that nagging hectic high
On that day where things should have gone right but didn't

I knew her.
Not like a wife and not like a mistress and different than a friend.
Although friends we certainly were.
She was there for me and I for her.
Whether it was for comfort or solitude or a quiet moment together
We would sometimes do the town. Take in some sights. A quiet restaurant
And we had our favorite. Where the staff knew you, but left you alone.
Where the menu was simple but the food like the old-fashioned diners.

After... we drifted back to her place and sometimes mine. I don't think it mattered but, on those nights, we slept intertwined.

Our love we seldom spoke of, as it knew no formalities like rings
Or contracts or titles of Mr. and Mrs. this or that.
Though our silent bond was stronger than any I've ever known and
She would tease of her illegitimate status and our unspoken roles
In this world that demands such formalities in order to label and
Categorize and define such things.
We refused to conform but knew our quiet reassuring love would last forever.
And it has. But now she smiles and teases and intertwines with me no more.
I long to be with her again. And I will. Soon, I think. And we shall laugh
And speak of our favorite table in our favorite restaurant and how we loved
And still love and no doubt always will.

She was beautiful
But not like a rose
For she carried no thorns and left no pricks as I
Stroked and caressed her sweet subtle form.
And so, she was much more than a flower I suppose
She was everything to me.

I Met A Girl

I met a girl. She takes my breath away
When she smiles that smile
I just don't know what to say
Her eyes sparkle and her laugh soothes my pain
I long for each moment
It's really hard to explain
I thought about telling her
Just how much I feel
Perhaps a few moments
She would allow for me to steal
To hold her close
And take in her scent
Make sweet love
That leaves us both spent.
I met a girl……

Those Who Have Never Loved

For those that have never loved
The love song has no meaning
For those that have never loved and lost
The sad song sings to an empty room
For those who have never cried in the waning hours
The poem drifts on past them
For those who've' never stared at a picture
Longing for the person in the familiar frame
They will never understand the pain and
How you will never be the same

Late at Night

I think of you late at night
When the moon is my only light
And the only sound is the low lazy
Whistle of a train far out of sight
I think about all the old, good times
The smiles and the laughs that seemed
To come so easily and without notice…
We had some fun
Didn't we?

Her Place

Met outside a dive called Sunset Bar
She needed a lift. I had a car.
Dropping easily into the custom leather seat
All curvy, vivacious, and some kinda sweet
Pulled out a cigarette with some funny sounding name
Brushed her thigh as I offered a flame.
Maybe twenty-nine or thirty.
Looked younger than her years.
Watched her closely while I worked through the gears.
Nothing said till her key fit the door.
Followed her in. Wanting to see more.
Small crowded space.
Not much more than a room.
She offered a drink. Gentlemen don't assume.
She on the couch. Me in a chair.
Thinking we're a most unlikely pair.
Stares piercing. Air stifling and still.
Taking it all in. I can't get my fill.
Her voice suggesting. Eyes locked.
World outside totally blocked.
Time melted in this quiet little place.
Smiled next day leaving.
On her peaceful sleeping face

As Time Creeps Up

As time creeps up on us and we begin to know
That our pain free days are few now and our hair the color of snow
We look back to reflect on life and what it all really meant
So many toils and troubles, so many blessings God has sent

It's easy to have misgivings, about what we did and didn't do
Every life has tough decisions and those you made make up you
So, we live with our regrets and thoughts of roads not taken
Try to worry not dear, over those you may have forsaken

Ease the mind of guilt and the memories bittersweet
Life is not really over, until God sees it as complete
Rest not on your laurels or what the past has brought us to
Look to today and tomorrow, for what it can give to you

Want

I want to kiss you...feel you…make your pulse race.
I want to squeeze you... caress you… enjoy your sweet taste.
I want to tease you... surround you… make your body squirm.
I want to finger you... lick you… press against you hard and firm.
I want to enter you... pulse in you... rock you till you cum.
I want to hold you... gently console you… listen to you sleep some.
I want to wake to you… laugh with you… watch the morning sun come up.
I want to hug you… walk with you… pour your morning cup.
I want to love you.

Searching

I searched for the perfect song to send you
Something that said what was on my mind
But it just wasn't there…
Then I tried putting some words together…
Something witty and clever and smart…
But the words didn't come.
I thought I'd talk about what I have been up to today…
But it all sounds trite and mundane…
So, I'm back to just thinking of you… and it takes me
Back to memories of your sweet smiling face…
And the feelings of warmth when I am close to you…
So, please just know darlin'…
That when you are on my mind…
I'm in a much better place.

Ghosts

My house is filled with ghosts
The strong wooden frames enshrine them
And take me back
As the past overtakes me... Memories rush in
Time stands still and I lose all track
There are my grandparents my uncles and a few lost friends
It's good to see them and I almost speak...
I miss their company and still tell their jokes
Sad to survive …. don't I wish for one more goodbye
The loss is painful even after all this time
If I don't get going, I'll stand here and cry
Enough for now, I really must go... But I promised them all
I would not forget
A promise I'll keep each morning... As I walk this hall

Late Night Dreamer

Sometimes late at night. In the wee hours of morning
I find myself wide awake dreaming. Thinking.
Reminiscing of various times of my past.
Of the few times I've actually loved.
Their smiling faces. The uniqueness that drew me to them.
The hard times and arguments fade away to nothing.
But the laughter, the closeness, and so many good times
Bring a smile to my lonely face.
Sometimes I think back to my service days.
The hardships, long hours, and challenges endured are
Diminished by the lifelong friendships, the interesting
Endeavors and places, I traveled that become more
Relevant and lasting in my memory.
Sometimes I drift back to the uncertainty of it all. Life.
So many ways it could have worked out.
But processing it all I realize
My late-night ventures into my past bring me to a
Certain conclusion and understanding.
Despite the scars inside and out
I have lived a life full of adventure, love, and experience
And for that I am thankful.
Let the tired sleep.
Let me dream awake.

Even Though

I stopped mentioning your name
Even though it's always on my mind.
I stopped eating at our favorite restaurant
Even though I walk past it often and stop to stare inside.
I stopped listening to our favorite song
Even though the lyrics still play to my ear
I stopped replaying your old phone messages
Even though they spoke directly to my heart
I stopped driving by our old house
Even though the happiest times of my life were spent there
I stopped reading your old letters
Even though they are all that sustains me
I stopped caring
Even though I know that's a lie.

If Life Was Simple

If only life was simple,
and dreams always came true,
if money were no object
there'd be so much to do...

If only time could stand still
when all was going great,
if only we were masters
of both our lives and fate.

If only everyone could smile,
at everyone they met.
If only we could wake each day
with nothing to regret.

If only it was easy
to always speak your mind.
Would life be much better,
is that what we would find?

If only I had taken time,
to do so many things...
spending time enjoying life
and everything it brings...

If only I had stopped to think
upon a time or two...
I might have changed a moment
if I'd only thought it through

The Days Are Long

The days are long
The nights seem longer
Smoke curls around my head as the gin turns stale
Nothing helps
My eyes rest behind dark shades allowing no one
To read the emptiness that resides within
I tell myself tomorrow will be another day. Better.
I know I am lying.
I should move. A change of venue. A different place.
What's the difference.
Without you I don't care.

It's Alright

It's ok. It will be alright
What I tell myself.
Often at night. When I'm alone.
And wondering.
If it really is and if it will be. Alright that is.
Strange. I was once so confident and sure of it all.
Then life happened. Or should I say death.
And the realization of how fragile everything is
Comes into focus and you're left wondering.
It will be alright. I say it again.
But I don't always believe.

Days and Nights

The days are long
The nights seem longer
I pray each night
That God makes me stronger
For the days are sad
And the nights are sadder
Sometimes I think
I just don't matter
Because the days are hard
And the nights are harder
Not sure I can endure
For very much longer
Since you went away
I've nothing much
to say
Except the days seem hollow
the nights seem black
And I can only think
How much I want you back.
The days. The nights.
They all run together.
What I wanted
Was Forever.

I Hear Your Thoughts

I hear your thoughts
and know your wants
I see the visions
that dance in your head
and feel the passion
forging you ahead.
I speak the music
of your soul
for in the heart
all is told.
Do not be
afraid of me
It is my love
that sets you free.

The Old Man

I stepped around him on a cold windy evening
His worn, tattered clothes and scraggly gray beard
Were out of place on this rather upscale business street
His hazy blue eyes stared off seeing nothing but the past
I stopped as I walked on by and for some odd reason
Turned and took another look at him.
Asking myself why …
Surely his whole life had not been spent in such a manner.
He probably once had friends. Family. A job maybe.
Perhaps a
Wife and even children.
What brought him here? Booze? Drugs? A bad turn or
A life altering event that he no longer could handle.
So, he dropped out of life's race… It's norms…
Perhaps not all at once but slowly. Over time.
He sunk deeper until no one cared. Especially himself.
I'm not sure and maybe at this point he no longer
Knows either. Survival his only focus, or maybe his
Next drink, a smoke or meal but certainly not much
beyond.
Feeling apathy or pity for him is normal I suppose.
But the thing that crept into my thoughts as I stood there
Looking back at him was one question.
How far is any of us from being him?
One bad turn.

Little Town Church

A long time ago in a little town church
Two young kids exchanged a vow...
A promise of love and lives to spend together
But that was then and this is now

Apprehensive but dreamy and still quite naive
Despite their inexperience, I truly do believe...
That the love they spoke of... was strong and true...
So who back then would have knew...
But that was then and this is now

Fate and destiny were not on their side
Promises made would later subside
Despite trying and crying and carrying on
It just wouldn't work and couldn't be won
But that was then and this is now

The boy went here... the girl went there
Separate lives lived, separate lives not shared
Decades pass and time keeps them apart
But something's missing from the lonely boy's heart
But that was then and this is now

Thinking back often as he dares sometimes allow
Drifting back to that past hallowed vow
Does she ever reflect on that little town church bell?
But that was then and this is now

Imperfect

Don' pick apart the individual notes dear one.
Don't dwell that it's a little off key.
Don't worry if it's a little out of tune sometimes.
Don't judge so close what you see.
Not much in the world is perfect.
Or could stand before an expert's stare.
What I've found in life most rewarding...
Was imperfect. but given with love and care

Another Time

Another time. Another place.
A curvaceous woman. With a beautiful face.
I reached out to her. And this is what she told me…
"I love you dear, but I'm setting your heart free".
What does that mean? What will I do?
In the end… It's not all left up to you.
It was only yesterday. It was long ago.
How could I possibly even know?
I've picked up the pieces. I've moved on.
Every now and then though, my mind goes gone…
To moments spent with her. And those blissful, timeless days.
Looking back, it was more than a life phase.
I'm fine. I'm alright. I'm doing well.
Forget I even mentioned it. Please do not tell.
But part of me will always be missing. Taken on that long-ago day.
I still thank God for her.
That's all that I can say.

The Girl in the Diner

She came in alone. Hesitant. Nervous it seemed
Casting eyes on everyone momentarily
Looking for someone
Sat in a booth two rows down
Facing me. Pretty but plain in all respects
Furtive looks to the counter and back to the door
Searching for someone or just watching out
Stayed over an hour at least
I drank several cups
Breakfast at dinner. These kinds of joints always have better breakfasts with real bacon
Stopped and asked her if she was alright on the way out
She looked down and nodded but a tear pooled at the corner of her eye
I walked out to the car. That was fall of 1979
Funny what events in life you remember and which ones you forget
I have often thought of the girl in the diner
What became of her and whether she found peace
Or answers.

V-day

Valentine's Day. I thought about a card.
Candy. Chocolate. Lingerie. A Rose….
So many options…
What man really knows?
My mind races to find an answer
Dining out, candlelight in…
I'm not really a dancer.
Somehow, I think they've lost the meaning
Hallmark. Fredrick's. FTD.
Hearts and flowers for all to see.
Not to appear cheap or insincere
I think I'll just whisper in her ear
A few simple words
Made explicit for hearts like mine
"I'll Truly Love You …for all my time."

The Flame

Those who are wise have said that the flame cannot
Outlast the candle ….
But my soul tells me that it can… and it does…
The torch burns on in the hearts of those who love.

Later Years

She lacked for nothing
But her possessions were few.
Rich in memories and experiences.
Of a past love who gave her everything
She would need to carry on
For her remaining days
A bittersweet existence of fond celebration
And looking back
To children now grown.
And a man now gone.

A Day in the Life

The day was beyond. The boss somewhat less than kind.
Staff shared their troubles. As if I had none of mine.
Stopped at my local. For a quick shot or a few.
Turns out they had a special. I told a story or two.
Left with a bit of a Sway. Not too steady on my feet.
Hit the empty side roads. Stayed off the busy main street.
Quietly I entered. Eased into bed.
Knew she was awake. But nothing to be said.
Like to say this day was the exception. But that would be a lie.
Mood seems to darken. Processing the how and why.
Changes in the wind.

One Short Life

We've all just one short life to live
Some seem to take... others choose to give
Some seek adventure, Some another way
Some live so long, some don't have long to stay
Some reach for knowledge, some don't seem to care
Some seem a bit stingy, some are willing to share
Some lose their direction, others seem to know
Some stay forever, others just up and go
Me I choose to ponder... just how it all works out
Perhaps knowing the answer, would relieve a lot of doubt

August Moon

Spent a week here by the wind the sea and fresh salty air
Leaving behind some homemade troubles and self-induced despair
Came to this island just to get away
That has since captured my soul… now wanting to stay

Found tranquility and comfort in this cozy bungalow
No doubt it's a refuge… for those feeling a little low
the water ripples against the quiet beach of August Moon
Indeed I wish to retreat back here again real soon.

Fifth of Nowhere

There's a place called a Fifth of Nowhere... a spot that I have been
It's somewhere half to Hell...and a little past Now and Then
You really don't want to be there. I'd prefer not to ever go back
Folks really aren't too friendly. Common courtesies they do lack.
I saw a man cry out there once. A poet that lost his rhyme.
It's just a place of transition, I guess. A place to spend some time.
Not sure how I even got there. My search for verse swept me along.
Surely, I'd be better off they'd say… if I'd learn to write a song.
But poems are my charge you see. It's a curse one falls into.
Just pray dear lord for sanity, and hope it won't happen to you.

In Plain Sight

Boobs come in all sizes... shapes... and condition
But regardless of shape… they all get our attention
Some point upward and some to the floor
Despite their direction …Guys love to adore
We like to ogle, squeeze, fondle and grope
When it comes to boobs... guys always have hope
Too bad many of them are kept wrapped up so tight
I'd like to see more of them out in plain sight.

An Ode to Jessie

I imagined for a minute that you were still here
And toasted my glass for all that could hear
Of the times that we shared and the stories that were told
With dear memories of yesterdays and years now old

I spoke of when you fished from deep outside the boat
As you found your glasses and wallet were not made to float
And the time you test drove my vehicle at speeds still unknown
As if the road was wide open and you were all alone

Rambling on then I raised my voice to deplore
How you drank at my table until a quarter till four
Dipping into my beer and taste testing my liquor...
Hanging on to the table till the dim lights began to flicker

I spotted you then in the corner with mug held high
Through smoke and silence as if to say goodbye
I nodded with a smile and beckoned with a call
Startled awake... you were gone... Nowhere at all
God rest your soul.

Remember

All your successes
And failures
In Life. Career. Relationships.
In the end
What's Important
Is who you have loved
How deeply you've loved
And who has shown you same
Who has touched your life
Made a difference
In the end
Your relationship with God
And all those you held dear
Is all that ever mattered.
Remember.

Christmas Blue

Christmas comes each year this time
Lights come out and the bells all chime
So much anticipation, so much glee
The holiday seems to set some people free

Free from daily hassle, free from struggled life
Suddenly forgotten is their trouble and strife
I seek shelter from this holiday
Looking for solitude and somewhere to stay

Being alone is just better for me
Not much one to mingle or sing by the tree
It's not that I'm a loner or a recluse by any means
Just no one to love or be close to it seems

I do not seek pity or sympathy from you
But if you happen to know someone else who is blue
Send them my way and I'll share with them my wine
And maybe we'll survive this holiday time

My Christmas Dream

Late Christmas Eve a light snow is falling.
My heart is aching yet no one is calling.
Where is my angel, my love, my soul.
It's midnight now I can hear the bells toll.

A strong wind picks up and I close my eyes.
When I open them, she's standing there to my surprise.
All my hopes and dreams wrapped up in this beautiful girl.
More beautiful than diamonds or the sea's rarest pearl.

She kisses me and all my pain and heartache float away
She seems uncertain but I ask her to stay
Lying then beside me all my wishes come true
I whisper, "my dearest, all I've wanted is you"
She says nothing; our bodies entwine
As our passion heats up, I pretend she is mine.

Tell Me

If I'm not what you want
Then why every time you think of me
Do your emotions run so strong
From a tear to fear
Of losing me or wondering if
I'm with someone else tonight.
If I'm not what you want
Then why do you constantly think of me
And want me near
If I'm not what you want
Then why do you cry for me dear
Your mixed messages drive me away
Why don't you just ask me seriously
Just please stay
If I'm not what you want
Just say so……

Coffee to Go

Night time goes so quickly
Daybreak and I'm up.
Stumbled to the kitchen
Lookin' for my cup.
Maybe today will be different
Things will take another turn
Off to work I'm headed.
A wage I've got to earn.
Bills they stand a waitin'
Sense of urgency they expound
Challenges at work await me
Opportunities do abound.
Like to think I'm earnest
Proud of what I do
Takin my coffee with me
And sweet thoughts of only you.

On the Counter

Coffee is good for thinking
It's also good for drinking.
I like to have me a bit
Sometimes just sip and sit
I appreciate early morning the most
I'll raise my cup in a toast.

Up and out too early
I've really not much to say
Staggered down the hall
I nearly lost my way
Needing coffee badly
I made the bathroom wait
If coffee is my destiny
I'll gladly accept my fate

Some say coffee is bad for you…
It makes you too uptight.
I've never been one to listen much…
I drink it day and night.
Some say it makes you nervous…
Some say it lifts you up.
I don't give a damn what they say…
As I pour another cup.

The Internet

It all comes down to just one thing
Whether to use Google, or Yahoo, or the infamous Bing
I once did a search on an unknown site
It left be bewildered and some kind of uptight
So, thought I'd venture out and ask Mr. Jeeves
He gave me the answer but then asked me to leave
I'm not so certain about all these "engines" on my net
They seem to have agendas and sometimes hedge their bet
So, I deeply researched this and thought carefully how to proceed
Typing my keyboard till my fingers did bleed
Come to the conclusion that one thing is set
You can't believe what you read…. On the internet.

Complaining

Complaining. All you hear
Human nature I suppose.
But it wears on you like a staticky radio.
Like a grumpy old man...
Non-stop with how it was in the "olden days"
A woman at the grocery about the price of milk...
Or a young kid who doesn't get what he wants
When he wants it.
I hear it in the store. In the street. Online.
I wonder if anyone stops to think anymore.
Of what they DO have. How many blessings bestowed.
How fortunate. How "rich" they truly are.
Probably not.
Human nature I suppose.

On Her Knees

I'm not sure why she's left me...
I'm not sure where'd she go
We once shared dreams together
I wish somehow I would know

Our relationship was based on freedoms
Founding principles etched in stone
I'd give my life to protect her
Despite troubles we have known

Once she cared and stood for honor
Pride shown in the way she lived
Now sadly she's lost direction
Nothing left in her to give

I watch as others now deface her
Taking the land between her seas
Can anyone please tell me
Why America is on her knees

Comfort

Give me the strength to go the miles
Down the road I know not where is going.
Let me see past the troubled reflections.
Let me dwell not on the crosses that must
Be Born.
And give me comfort in the knowledge
That the street I'm on has an end.

CPSIA information can be obtained
at www.ICGtesting.com
Printed in the USA
BVHW031115250719
554364BV00009B/109/P